It's often said that a man is but a sum total of his thoughts, ideas, emotions, feelings, influences, and experiences. Tony, what thought, what idea, what emotion, what feeling…what a man!
—*The Honorable Lynn K. Stewart, Judge—Circuit Court for Baltimore City; Baltimore, Maryland*

"Enthralling! This neophyte work captivates with the commanding tenor of a seasoned voice."
—*Iva Ferrell, Associate Counsel—QVC Inc.*

"Emotionally passionate, a unique perspective from the male point of view."
—*Kim Beamon, Author—"The Game" and "If Cubicles Could Talk"*

"All authentic writers are born liars and truth-tellers at the same time. All fiction is lies, and all fiction is true. Tony Johnson is a "liar" of the highest order—he tells the truth."
—*Rebecca Williams, Evergreen Writers*

"Tony Johnson is a vividly passionate writer/poet. With rapt intensity, he beckons the reader along a continuum spanning from captivating intrigue to beguiling machination."
—*Cinda Gaskin, Publishing Manager*

That's It!

That's It!

Thoughts of Fantasies, Half-Truths, and Outright Lies

A Collection of Poetry and Short Stories

A.P. Johnson

Writers Club Press
New York Lincoln Shanghai

That's It!
Thoughts of Fantasies, Half-Truths, and Outright Lies

Writers Club Press
an imprint of iUniverse, Inc.

For information address:
iUniverse
2021 Pine Lake Road, Suite 100
Lincoln, NE 68512
www.iuniverse.com

Any resemblance to actual people and events is purely coincidental.
This is a work of fiction.

Edited by
Marie Joyner Corniffe,
Nina Stewart, and Rosalind Murphy

Cover Art by
KDL Graphics—Laurel, MD.

ISBN: 0-595-24483-1

Printed in the United States of America

In Remembrance:

Angela C. Johnson—Mother, Teacher and Encourager.

Contents

Contents

Acknowledgments

To God for providing each day. To my M&Ms for providing the inspiration that keeps me moving forward. To my family for being a sounding board, even when they didn't want to listen. To Majoco's Collections—Plainfield, for having open mic at the right time. To Marie and Ralph, John Scipio, Margie Shaheed, Dr. Jerry Gant, Pink Diamond, Mar Hill, Roz, Felicia and Charles, Serengeti Plains—Montclair, Euphoria Café—Newark; the African Globe Theatre—Newark, and all the Poets, Writers, Spoken Word Artists and Fans throughout New Jersey.

To all my alter-egos, Anthony, Tony, Trick, AJ, and TJ for each of their own unique voices, personalities, and views of the world.

And lastly, my fantasies, the muse when all else fails.

AP Johnson

Introduction

…and when the world was wrong, my grandma made it right, she made things ok for them, just like she did for me.

—"Never Cried"

I believe everyone needs a "someone". A someone who will make the world alright. A someone who will believe in you, encourage you, and hug you when no one else in the world will.

Everyone has someone who can take away some of the pain, who can make some of the things ok. But I was blessed to have someone who could take away all of the pain.

For me, it was my grandmother. Whether she was baking me bread, playing pitty pat or gin rummy, or very simply reminding me of the things I could do, she was the light behind the dark clouds.

She couldn't help being that way, her name was Christmas; Ernestine Christmas, my "Mama Stine". And just like the holiday, being with her was always a joy. So when she passed, it was as if Christmas itself had been taken from me. It was like a true to life version of the Grinch came into my life and stole the dearest one to me. Life became a bit cloudy, the sun wasn't as warm, and the stars didn't seem to shine as bright. I was holding on to something that I couldn't get out. Then by accident, or maybe subconsciously on purpose, I stopped by Majoco's Collections in Plainfield when they just happened to be having an open mic poetry reading. I listened and heard love, hurt, pain, and joy.

I started writing. Eventually I had a piece here, a piece there. Emotion started leaving me and getting onto the paper and the clouds started to break. Stars got their twinkle back and the sun had warmth.

From that period came "Never Cried", a "mostly truth".

"That's It!", is truly filled with thoughts of fantasies, half-truths, and outright lies. It's snapshots of emotions and feelings; some felt, some seen, and some avoided. But life is emotion, and emotion makes up lives…hey, THAT'S IT!

I. Talk is Cheap

Truth is housed by the tellers
like the bank, only being able to
withdraw a bit at a time
and when your truth runs out,
you're overdrawn
and no trust will give you a loan
and now I'm not sure
just what is the truth

CheapPen

I bought a cheap pen and wondered if the cheap pen would
    write cheap words
that tell cheap stories.

Would it prevent me from carrying you away on my winged
    words to the sun
or would the cheap pen's words melt like waxed wings in the
    heat
dashing us back to our earthly realities?

Would the cheap words fit like a cheap suit you bought at a
    cheap store,
Made from cheap wool, shorn from a cheap sheep
or cheap cotton grown in a cheap field, picked by cheap labor?
You could wear it a few times but the cheap threads holding it
    together,
like this prose, would soon begin to tatter.

Are cheap words filled with empty promises
or are they used to bandage broken dreams?
And in those dreams, are cheap themes used as replacements?

Did the cheap pen cheapen the motivation
and simply write cheap answers that cheapened others?
rather than asking the real questions of value to yourself?

After a cheap date could you get cheap sex?
And would that be fulfilling or just a cheap thrill?

Were cheap thoughts created in the cheap side of the mind?
Could those cheap thoughts be enhanced by a few shots of
    cheap booze

or a cheap 40?
and if you drank too much of the cheap stuff,
would you become a bit too drunk...
or a 2 bit drunk?

Did the cheap pen have cheap ink?
And did cheap ink run out any faster?
And if so, would *you* buy another cheap pen?

If the pen was as cheap as I thought it was,
did that mean I could possibly write a check that my cheap
    ass couldn't cash?
Or did I buy the cheap pen to write cheap words because I
    knew,

TALK IS CHEAP!

Words

Words on this page are somewhat complementary
Complementary to one another
They are catalysts for continuing
and the foundation that magically
transforms a blank page and an open mind
into alluring inviting sentences
They are the metaphorical bulldozer
pulling emotions and pushing visual descriptions
transcending physical realities
and harsh half-non-truths
offering insight
Insight into the feelings of the author
They add to the virtual screenplay
The hope for a happy ending
The hope for a new beginning
The hope that the passion for life prolongs death
The words invite supplemental words
needed for meaning and completion
Words build into phrases offering meaning
And because of the words on this page
We will transcend our differences
And you and I will be momentarily connected.

I Want to Blow You Away

I want to blow you away with words
Words once heard in the Hanging Gardens of Babylon
Words that pound your soul like the beat of a tribal drum
Words that heat you up like the Sahara at midday and
Then cool you down like the breezes atop Kilimanjaro

I want to blow you away with passion
Passion grown only in the Nile Valley
The passion and power of Ramses and Osiris
The passion of the builders of the Pyramids and Temples
Who took architecture and mathematics, and created the
    impossible

I want to blow you away with understanding

I want to blow you away with compassion

I want to blow you away with feelings

The feeling you had when you first fell in love for the first time

Passing of a Soul Brother!

I used to pass by my soul brothers regularly.

Now I avoid the places where "da brothas" hang out.

We'd see each other and smile; he'd say "What's happening my man? Yeah, right on. Cool. Slap me five!"

Now it's, "Hey where you think you goin'? What you lookin' at? You better step off fo you get slapped."

He'd say, "How's your mother?", or "How's the family doing?" Now it's "Yo mama ain't...", or "She's a..."

He'd say, "Hey man, you need a ride?" Or, "I'm going to the store, what do you need?"

Now he takes my car in the night while I sleep, or in broad daylight, at gunpoint if necessary.

He was always there; where and when I needed him.

Now, I never know where or when I'll run into him. When I do, my body tightens, wondering if it's my turn, if I'm his latest mark.

And when we passed, he'd say, "Catch you later", or "See you later Blood."

Now when we pass I wonder if we'll ever pass again, and if so, will one of us be covered with blood?

I used to have soul brothers in my neighborhood.

Now I just have hoods!

Lust After Love

I am powerfully affected by love
every time it shows itself to me
which is funny
because I am totally incapable of
loving

I learned early that
everything has strings attached
yet the math still don't add up
attraction acted on…plus time,
equals love…
which is greater than or equal to
lust

Things got convoluted as
the integral parts of relationships
from lust to attraction;
when systematically removed
or when run of its course
yields the end of friendships,
breakups and
in extreme cases,
something less than or equal to
divorce

There's no relation
that this correlation
got screwed up
it's all mixed up
all this time thinking
"This must be love!"

Wrong,
because the fire burning
was lust
so lust equals love…right?
that must be what all the
love hub-bub is about

Now I stand crippled before you
like a eunuch
castrated by memories
lusting through trusts
inaccurately postulating theorems
that manhood
was measured in
quantities of sex

And here's the irony
the pushers weren't my boys
pushing me towards joy
with cheers of
"Go get'em boy!"
No, it was the ladies.
Enablers;
co-sponsoring my addiction
feeding my lust
who do you trust?
fueling my dependence
by letting me know
it was ok to play
if I was paying…
Paying for dinner, or movies;
for flowers, shoes, or jewelry

Fancy women with
casual glances, winks and smiles
leading to contact while dancing
setting the rules we all could play by
"YOU GOTTA JOB?"
"WHEN YOU GONNA TAKE ME OUT?"
Ready to collect and serve
choosing to cash in around GO
material games
when loving me
should have been about
emotional gains
about partnerships and planning
about vacations and tanning
about suburbs and picket fences…
about us as best friends

Who can be friends
at a time like this?
Lights all turned out
scented candles burning
kisses and nibbles
while zippers unzipping
buttons unbuttoning
grinding and thrusting
moans, whispers, lust
lust moans and whispers…
"Make love to me"
I think I'm falling in love

LUST!

Measuring Honesty

If honesty were measured
how much would do?
A dab, a pinch, or a sprinkle?

How much would you need
for baking the nourishment of love that
your body needs to grow?
A teaspoon, a tablespoon, or a handful?

How much honesty would you need
to find the peace and comfort you long for?
Would you measure it in a cup, or two?

After cooking on heat too high
and baking my words for far too long
you have burned them into nothingless meanings
words now fail to rise from your sour yeast
your recipe has grown old
yet you blatantly ignore the spores
throwing another batch in the oven of
molding insecurity and fear

I've come to the conclusion that my honesty
is increasingly under your suspicion
and that doesn't stand to reason
the further we have gone
the more questions I seem to get
the batter of this relationship has lumps
and it's left me unfulfilled, malnourished and compromised

You measure honesty by
tracking and tracing my steps because you lack faith

never gave you a reason for distrust
yet your mind continues to cook rotten cuisine,
rationalizing that your inability to completely control me,
means you can't trust me

You can't trust me out of your sight
and question my every move
And, funny, the more you try to leash me
and boil me into your web of control and submissiveness
because of your lack of social esteem
the more I realize too many kooks spoil the soup

You measure honesty in pints, pints of my answers for
where I'm going, where I've been or what time I'll be home
You measure honesty in quarts, quarts of how well
my boy's answers will match mine after a poppin' fresh quiz
on our where-bouts over 6 weeks ago

And, time after time I've passed your tests
I've passed your honesty quizzes and drills
your incessant search for the truth,
the truth that simmers right beneath your eyes
the truth that you search for like a "60 Minutes" producer

My honesty continues to lead
to your actions of further questioning me
because of the hurt you've received from others in the past
That hurt has you unable to trust me
as I lay with you, committed to our future

Your reaction is the lightning and thunder creating havoc
in an otherwise sweet spring shower
the storm within makes you restless in the night

it causes you to wake crying
looking for my shoulder to lean on
because you love me and
you need me to be there for you
to hold you
yet you scream each day to get the hell out
because you got your own, and you don't need no man

Honestly, I'm tired of measuring the talk of honesty
talk—talk—talk about talking
I'm talking about the future
the future that is tomorrow
cause we can't change your past
and I damn sure can't help you get over the dishonesty
that you're not willing to let go of

Honestly, I no longer want to be the subject of your nocturnal
      inquisitions
your irrational images based in the lucid dreams of your
      growing insecurity
suddenly, the image of a stallion running free
seems like the a-la-carte choice for me

Measure this:
If you ain't
Good to me
Good with me
Good for me
I'm gone!

Honestly

Temporarily Insane — used the wrong brain

Hey mama…mami, que pasa?
How you doin?
Hey baby can I get those digits?
Yo, you looking good
Daaaaammmmnn, ain't you fine
What's your name?
I'd like to get to know you better…

Sound like a bunch of lines? They're all lines.
"Hello, how are you?" sounds like a line
when you don't want to be bothered

I will tell you everything you want to hear…
No woman has ever asked for more than I could promise!
And guess what? Shhhhh, I *have* promised the world.

I will tell you I'll do all those things for you
As long as it gets me what I want. And tonight I want you.

OK…I admit it, I'm guilty, I'm temporarily insane. But I blame
    you.
The way you look at me, the way you smile, the way you
    smell…
I became light headed. All the blood rushed from one head to
    the other
It took away all my ability to reason and use of my common
    sense—I'm sure you could tell

That's It!

I'm temporarily insane. The verdict fits, I cannot deny
Surely there's no reasonable doubt, you have to see what you
    do to me
You're so intelligent, you're so beautiful, and your voice so
    soothing
At the risk of being embarrassed, you know I had to try

I'm temporarily insane, but then again, I'm just a man!

A Storm is Brewing

A storm is brewing
clouds on the horizon
thick and full of static anger
black and non-white
powerful clouds
all shapes, shades,
sizes and colors
trumpeting trouble
ready to attack
with electric blasts

Black lightning
unseen in the night
strikes fast
destroying Miranda Rights
thunderous rumblings
loudly yelling,
stay the hell out of our way
we're coming through
lightning unseen
crackling and booming
like woofers
that bounce butterflies
out of your stomach
and straight to hell
during drive-bys
woofers that keep the beat
of the mac, ak, or any semi-auto gats

as the streets empty quickly
like "Dodge City"

A black storm
is brewing
getting so Black it's light
and Black outs
are going to eradicate
those who try to
keep people away
from truth and justice
as it breaks
those good-ole boys'
"American Way"
of inequality and inopportunity
of glass ceilings
poorly supplied schools
and second class looks
from those
who are the true crooks

This storm is growing
it's going to be big
it's off the radar
and "Twister" will
seem like a day in the park
it's filled with power
more powerful
than a strobe lit trooper
doing 105 on 95
looking to fit
a profile for DWB

near exit 3
or drop a bag at the
scene if need be
if your profile fits
the jury won't acquit
the officer was justified
with probable cause!
and it's sure hard to get
to work without a
license.

Where is the millennium
"King" to sing psalms
to cleanse those
in need of calm
or sing songs that unify
black clouds
and focus storms into
cooling sprinkles
that fall like snow on cotton
that turn dry baked farms
back into fertile minds

Where is the millennium
"X" to vex this hex
and wake up
all the sleepwalkers
and show these mean acts
we have endured are
the means to bring
the downpour necessary
and carry the storm

straight to the doors of those
who need reform
so they can and will see
if you ain't with us
you must be against us!
and we all intend to be free

This is Not a Slam Poem!

This is not a slam poem
so don't score me
I'm not going to stand here
and lie
or give you lines about
how much I love you
or how much you hurt me
I won't talk about times
filled with crazy hot lustful sex
I won't talk about how you look
or how you lick or
the sweetness that you drip
or throw in double entendres
about my stick
I won't even discuss
late night booty call hits
no matter how good I was!

This is not a slam poem
I won't scream about oppression
for 4-or-500 years
about how drums in another land
and another time cry tears and
beat the same beat my heart beats today
about how my red blood is traced
to my darkest ancestors
albeit denied and concealed by my fair skin
I won't make rap songs about my succession
from the hood, getting up and out
while leaving some behind with the

nickel, and dime bags I sold them
back when I was "thugged out!"

This is not a slam poem
I won't yell epitaphs on Ephesians
or quote Psalms of praise to the Almighty
He who rules and guides my faith
and from whom all blessings flow
I won't say "God is good"
expecting you to come back with
"All the time"
all the time knowing inside
"if I get the crowd repeating me,
my score will be higher"

This is not a slam poem
cause I don't intend to learn it
word for word
I don't intend to recite or perform it
so it can be judged against scores
by people at random
based on visual stimulation
opposed to the merits of words;
their form, their style,
or my verbal manipulation
…and it's definitely not a slam poem
cause anyone who gets up to slam
and talks about Sex, Drugs,
Oppression or a Deity with shocking content
and choreographed physical dexterity
will win!…

So please don't expect to hear a slam poem from me!

Can I Say I Miss You?

Knowing not
care less or do;
my connection remains strong
seeing you when I do
you hardly know me
share words, "how are you?"
Can I say, I miss you?

Sight of mine
follows you on your way
words fumble and mumble,
know not what to say
glance from afar
watching legs, hips they sway
please understand,
I miss you.

Lo, My Heart

Lo, my heart has been lifted
Lifted from the depths of the cold hell it was banished to
Depths deep as night is dark
The darkness of loneliness
Pushed away by the dirty hands of the uncaring
Beaten by the heartless and savagely torn by the greedy

Lo, my heart has been lifted
Lifted from beneath this concrete mausoleum called hatred
From the catacombs as cold and biting as a December rain
Taking the sweetness of life and sapping it
Sapped like a maple, drained of its last drop of sweetness

Lo, my heart has been lifted
Lifted from this earth of sadness and grief
Sad as a tree uprooted after a raging storm
Lost as the kite un-tethered in the wind
Forgotten like the today's news on the last train's tracks

Lo, my heart has been lifted
Beautifully lifted like the jewel on Ra's staff
Strongly lifted like the capstone atop the Great Pyramid of
    Cheops
Safely lifted in the hands of care and kindness with the touch
    of acceptance

Lo, my heart has been lifted
Gently lifted by unconditional love.

Spoil Me

Spoil me with your eyes
eyes that look beyond physical beauty
past all of my imperfections
eyes that aren't afraid of what they might see!

Spoil me with your mind
a mind filled with self-confidence
open and uninhibited without hang ups,
expectations, or judgments
a mind that challenges me to think

Spoil me with your tongue
the tongue that has tasted the salt of my tears,
the salt of my toils, and the salt of my being
the tongue that has formed the words,
I love you!

Withdrawal

Can you feel the rain as it falls on you?
it's clear;
cold drops smart like small smacks
when it's really a big whack you need
to get yourself up and going again, and again
all senses are lost when the mind has been
retarded, dulled and stored away on a mental break
from the broken heart that won't stop pounding,
beating and screaming in your ear "I told you so"

Can you stand the pain through the numbing rain
that has replaced the fleeting joy in you?
now that you clearly see the pounding rush of energy
that woke you up and pushed you daily through another day
like a nonstop mainline hit of hot caffeine is gone
leaving only the bitter grounds remaining
while the cream sours at the top
and all the sugar in the world won't make it sweeter

Do you even care what tomorrow holds for you,
when you don't even know what day today is?
as your body shakes and you cry uncontrollably
robbed of your feelings of care, tenderness and compassion
fighting through the withdrawals of love
alone, alone, alone.

Questions for God

Did the original caveman know about God?
Did he question his being? Wasn't it odd
That he should be here on earth and walking so free
With dinosaurs, his cave-woman, and forests and streams?

Who did he pray to? What wisdom was imparted?
Did worshiping fire cause aches when we started?
Were the heartaches much more than we suffer today?
Was ancient man damned before Moses gave way?

If it was a mistake, as God realized,
to hurt his own people with floods or a fire
Couldn't it be argued that Eve too was weak
and made a mistake in the yard with that snake?
Possibly, you'd think that we'd all be forgiven
Instead of the strife in this life that we're living

Africa, the cradle of civilization, producing world knowledge
was stolen by Romans and others for dollars?
Tell me what brown people have done to deserve all of this?
To be sold into slavery and continually oppressed?

If Jesus, as man, came to save all our souls
And died for mankind, as all Christians know
Why do we continue to suffer these blows?
Why is there hell on this earth God? I must know.

And what about all the religious fanaticals
More willing to fight so they can kill other radicals
Wasn't religion supposed to save all the meek?
Who's going to heaven, the Klan in their sheets?

That's It!

And why are some priests who seek your applause
Hiding under robes as they chase alter boys
Hiding behind pulpits in the name of God
as they control people's lives, now isn't that odd?

And ministers who scream, yell and sweat in Your name
Are chasing young girls with thoughts of the same
Or getting caught with their hands in the till
Be it money or sex, they're all scandals still

If made in Your image, we are as man
What is that image? Please tell me, You can
Is it the beauty the inspired can choose to create?
Or is it the ugliness the ignorant destroy with their hate?

If You are omnipotent You must be within us
So reach us and teach us the lessons of justice
Give me the strength to search one more day
For the reason we still all kneel when we pray.

II. Mind Dances

It's been too quiet here
if you know what I mean
I expected for earths to quake
and volcanoes to shake
I expected blizzards to blow
to see folks stuck in snow
to hear winds howl by
and deserts to stay dry
to hear that peace was on earth
and man was now recognized by his
internal self-worth
I expected that children would stop crying
and men would stop fighting
that everything would be alright in the end…
But it's not…
is it?

Reflections

Spoken words in empty clubs
fall silent like tears through eyelashes.
Background beats on high-hats tick
like seconds on the clock
reminding time to march on

mirrors only reflect the reflections of themselves
mirrors reflect only the reflections of themselves
mirrors reflect the reflections only of themselves
only mirrors reflect the reflections of themselves
and isn't that redundant?

Writer's Block

The umbilical cord
between creative cognizance
and manual dexterity
has been severed
through to the optical nerve

I recall images of beauty
and colorful scenes
but they won't translate
into legible words
as I bleed blue blood
on dry lined paper

Intelligible thoughts
crowd mindscapes
stuffed and packed
by gargoyles and nightmares
pushing thoughts;
too many thoughts, so fast
they blur and defy description
like ghosts
unwilling to be discovered

Madman

Eyelids drop, heavy from the weight
as if they've seen enough
this life, tough as it seems
sometimes not worth living, but
it's still better than the alternative

Rubbing 'til they burn
rubbing more to stop the burn
red stares and screams greet passers-by
yawns are the only thing now
that stop the babbling of this madman

Daytime Moonbeams

It's funny that moonbeams
become dust in the daylight
chased and swept with a broom
so a 3 dimensional square,
a cube—called a room
will be clean

Nocturnal screens reveal scenes
of dreams through stars
though, there all the time
hidden by rays of days
with spotless cubes...
so where is a dream to reside?

The darker the shade
the more that's revealed
like a shroud or a cape
in the expanse
of a pitch unknown
a frontier that's final
yet infinite...
so too the possibilities
of moonbeams dreams

It's funny how
dust is despised
and disposed during days
while, every child
looks to collect
moonbeams in their pockets
to fly from the finite fate
of dust-balls under beds

Euphoria

Candles flickered slowly and
bathed the room in soft colors;
their scent was vanilla.

Couples coupled
as they spoke in whispers
above the ti, ti, ti,
rhythm ticks of the drummers beat
on the stereo and the swishing sound
of latte steaming into hot espresso.

Word artists and music makers
gathered hoping their tunes
and sonnets would move,
would inspire
the packed, crowded room.

Artists all
fought to control
their natural butterflies
and caught their breath
as they made their final preparations.

The first cat up
spoke of young revolution…
"it's our time now!", he chanted.
Heads young and old nodded in agreement.

Next, a woman sang a sad song.
A song so sad, tears rolled down her face.

The silence and awe
were broken by thunderous applause.

One after another,
each artist rolled to the mic
full of energy
and gave all of themselves
in hopes of capturing
a momentary connection
with the audience.

The night grew late,
but talent rolled on strong;
each one as impressive as the last.

When the night ended,
after the crowd had gone,
the artists hugged and kissed
and praised their respect and love
for each other's work.

Emotion and collective creative energy
filled the room.
And for a moment—one small moment…
no one had any problems!

Is There a Poet in the House?

Is there a Poet in the house?
Quick, I need a pad and a pen.
This fever just came over me
sweating like it's 95 degrees outside
but freezing with goose bumps
POET…heal thyself!

I just got a twinge
not sure if it's my head
or my heart…again.
But it's cool,
cause that's when
poets mend their cuts, bruises and hurts
into prose and spoken thoughts
like some kind of psychological band-aid.

All that deep down stuff
you don't want to talk about
with anyone
suddenly pops out
like the Prozac and Valium tabs
that drop from your pocket
when your looking for change

Don't patronize me
with your ooohs, aaahs,
and I'm so sorrys
just give me a damn pad and a pen.
Don't you realize
the longer you sit there
analyzing me,

the less chance there is
for any meaningful prose
to materialize or survive?

I'm battling for my sanity
this is a fight
and I'm determined to
wrestle these psychotic demons to
penned verbal thoughts
give me a pad and a pen, now!
Is there a Poet in the house?

Insomnia

Not sleeping is common
it's now the norm
a state I visit nightly
as I toss and turn
torn by the thorns of your
rosy disposition
each night
hearing wind whispers,
watching stars shine
and lightning bugs flitter
while cars on the move
can't stop crickets or critters
from buzzing in my ear

Searching for silence
solitude in my bed
tracing long gone steps
running around in my head
trying to determine the answers;
what's right?
my brain starts to race
flashing visions of yesterdays
reliving conversations that maybe
could have been better said
or better yet left unsaid
remembering thoughts of last words
after they slip past protected gates
of tightly pursed lips
and unable to pull them back
ignited by the instigating black magic
burning inside you

With my eyes shut tight
I cross my feet and
squeeze my thighs
hoping tonight will be the night
that I can squeeze enough to
brake this insanity
tight enough to find relief
squeezing so tightly my feet tingle
from the numbness of constricted flow
hoping the physical pain
will finally give me peace
as I grind my jaw to migraines
and my stomach cramps
beneath my arms
corseting my ribs
hugging me longing for the comfort
that will rock me
off to sleep

Right Minded

Incense filled the room to
cover the bone she just smoked.

Dark glassy eyes looked across the room
smooth jazz—a Spanish mandolin fluttered in the background.

She was nervous…
no one was talking
She found a piece of paper
And carefully folded it again and again
To pass the time.

She didn't know what to do
She didn't know what to say
All she knew is that she was in the right mind.

The right mind—Released from the day's pressures and troubles
The right mind—Released from the thought of tomorrow.
The right mind—Ready to love tonight.
The right mind—Ready to love…Right Now!

Shards

Warming the body
with tingly pins
and bringing the smile,
the sustenance of life.
It pounds through the temples
driving migraines to the sane
and sleepless insomniacs
to the point of insanity
all the while
boring its way to the jugular

Dropped, put down
pushing another shard
into this shattered life
Shattered shards of broken glass
cut arteries as the heart pumps beat
bum—bump
bum—bump
bum—bump

Despite that I reach out to you
again and again…thinking…
If your hand was mine to hold
and my shoulder was yours to lean on
would you feel what I feel?

If you knew all there was to know
and felt all there was to feel
would you know this feeling
yet and still?

And knowing all of this
and feeling all of this
would you stop the shards
that shatter lives
bum—bump
bum—bump
bum—bump

Before this heart stops

The Last Game

It was a hot day with barely a warm breeze. The sun baked the blue-white cloudless sky. Everything was still except for three hawks that silently soared in circles, high above the corn stalks looking for a field mouse or two. I had been here for what seemed like an eternity, silent, careful not to make a sound. I was determined that they wouldn't find me. I had built a strong reputation and I wasn't going to let it down today. I had been at it for a while, my cunning and my speed kept them at bay and allowed me to escape several close calls. I had come up through the ranks with the best of them and watched them all—one by one get knocked off while they were at the top of their game, even saw some of my best buddies caught. I couldn't help them or say a word for fear of disclosing my position. It was now up to me, I was the last one.

They were dead on my tracks. It was as if they knew every move I would make before I made it. They had been chasing me for so long, I think they were beginning to think like me and they were finally closing in. I had ditched them earlier, when I saw them in front of the house, I ran behind it, when their focus was distracted, I ran and somehow made it to the barn undetected. The old red barn was nothing more than a big storage shed with horse stalls, a few hay wagons, and a gigantic loft full of hay. The doors of the barn had worn from a lifetime or two of wear and tear, so there were small open cracks that I could peak through without being seen.

As I looked out I could see several old rusty abandoned cars in the corner of the field, the old out-house, and a feed silo. I could see them looking around, talking, and then pointing towards the barn. They began making their way towards me. How could they know I was here, they didn't even bother to check the other things in the field?

I was getting that "trapped mouse" feeling and began to look around for a place to hide. I was beginning to sweat from the heat and from feeling cornered. I had to get a grip on the situation, had to pull myself together if there was any hope for escape. There was a ladder that led to the loft. I jumped up the ladder and quickly moved to the back corner. I quietly propped several bails of hay around me to stay out of sight and squatted down just as the big barn doors creak open.

I focused for an escape. The sun was bright and peeked through several holes in the weather worn roof. Dusty sunbeams danced up from the floor as the group walked in. It was hot and dry in the loft. I wiped the sweat away from my eyes and looked through the cracks of the bails. The group looked for me in each stall and I could hear the leader, the biggest one, talking from the corner just beneath me. I heard him tell one of the guys to go up the ladder and check the loft.

I had to think quickly, had to find a way out. I reached down and felt my pockets...I grabbed a few pennies out and flung them against the old, dry wooden wall in the opposite corner of the barn. They all ran to see where the noise came from. As their backs turned, I made a dash for the loading window and jumped onto one of the hay wagons below and took off running, practically before my feet hit the boards. They heard my body land on the wagon. The momentary confusion was broken when the big guy yelled, "There he is...get him!"

I ran as fast as I could, dust puffing up like smoke clouds with each step driving into the ground, legs pumping like a steam engine. I ran. I could hear their steps behind me, not closing in, yet not getting further away, just the constant thump, thump, thump, thump...they seemed to be running in unison. My breaths quickened. I knew if I made a few hundred more yards, I'd be free. They wouldn't be able to touch me in the free zone. Just ahead, just ahead I focused and ran, I ran. I don't know which was louder, my heart thumping or the thumping of the feet behind me. I ran, I can't remember breathing, I just ran.

I reached the big tree in the front of the house and fell forward too tired to take another step. I rolled onto my back, my chest heaving up and down gasping for air, my lungs gasping…for oxygen.

HOME-FREE, I yelled in between breaths, just as the group caught up to me. They were shocked, they stood around me with their mouths open in a combination of surprise and trying to catch their breaths. No one had ever been able to get away every time. Never! They always got their man, until this time. I laughed. They knew this was their last chance for the summer. They began to laugh too. We'd all have to go in soon and I'd be on a plane back home tomorrow. For now, I just sat back and smiled and enjoyed the moment. Summer was ending, and for now, at least until next summer, I was the farm's hide-&-seek legend.

Wind

Blowing nor'easter winds
gale school doors shut
grandmas turn off TVs and lights
as the city goes dark
keep quiet, cause it's the Lord's time

Winds blow spirits of bar room poets
ripping thoughts from their hands
blowing clear the cigarette smoke
freeing the minds of those who have seen
while we bask in the shade of hidden truth

Winds turn the bible pages
of street corner preachers who yell
"God is watching"
while across the street the Muslim minister
tells the so-called,
"Be not fooled by the hidden work of the devil"
as he works to keep his Final Call pages from flying

I fly through the air
on the winds of poets past
no fear of falling
yet I cannot land
I am not grounded by gravity or lies

The winds blow my words into twisters
twisting meanings into unfocused understanding
of what I'm trying to say
I confuse you with

superfluous agitated prose,
biting truth, and dangling participles

I speak in circles
tossing prepositional phrases
asking for visions of thoughts
locked in illusions
and have the nerve to say
you know?
As the bar room fills with smoke

Literary Voyeur

I sit back and watch
waiting for your name
to appear in the "from" line
I look at your words
marching across the screen
like literary Morse-code
and visualize you
sitting and writing them

seeing your words appear
signals the synapse of joy and fear
to begin their tango
in my chest and in my head
I am under your spell

I have come to
learn your emotions
one letter at a time
smiles—laughs
fears and tears
all in black type
while the white glow
basks my face

I know you and you don't know me
I know you and yet we've never met
I know you, I'm your literary voyeur

In the darkness of my room
I see your lines
not your curves

yet I'm aroused
I sit and virtually listen
as you talk just to me
I am aroused by your mind
and your capacity to
create and stir emotions within me

and I grasp my heart
as my emotions fight within
thinking of the next time
I'll see you again
I'm your literary voyeur
and you will never know me

Last Time Again

I thought about you
last night
for the last time
again
and through this mental block
I tried hard to define
the reason
I needed to find
to find
the cause

I paused
wondering if it was
a scent?
a color?
or whispers of some tune
that got me in the mood
that flashed me back
to visions of you
I stood stunned
I meant never to have
you on my mind
again

I'm fine
moving on by myself
doing the things I told you
I need to do
when suddenly it disturbs me
that hanging out with my crew
doesn't seem as fun
as hanging around with you.

Peace

A body reaches high on the shelf of life
It's an upward climb on the stair-master
Each step taken, no closer to peace.

Reach higher, it's just beyond the finger tips
So close you can touch it
So far that touching it pushes it further away.

Doesn't peace need rest?
Doesn't peace want to rest here?
Isn't this body deserving of the quiet?
The weary flesh and bones are longing for it.

STILL reaching till the arm cramps,
STILL reaching till the fingers tingle,
STILL reaching till the tip toes ache.

Soul screams; raw nerves refuse to numb…life's pain
The drugs won't let me forget
The drugs won't ease the pain

Muscles now refuse to respond
No way to reach higher
Muscles constricted and cramping
It looks so far away

Undeniable…will broken…acceptance…complete;
Embracing the inevitable

And just like that…it comes,
peace…

Rain

(music plays)—Bill Withers
Ain't no sunshine when she's gone
It's not warm when she's away
Ain't no sunshine when she's gone
And she's always gone too long
Anytime she goes away

Wonder this time where she's gone
Wonder if she's gone to stay
Ain't no sunshine when she's gone
And this house just ain't no home
Anytime she goes away

It rains sheets in Philadelphia
And I still hear Butterball or the Dr.
And "Still-Bill"
Withers moist soul on the radio

Drops splash the window, wild wind biting
Sounds like fingers tapping on the table in staccato
While the distant thunder
Keeps the beat

Rain is good for growing dreams
Inside dreams…collections and recollections of scenes
All that has been, dreams of what could be
And wondering what it all means

Good for cleansing, and washing away the deep
Thoughts you no longer want or need to keep

Streams surge rushing away things left outside
Without a peep

Good for sowing what you may reap
Planted thoughts within the fertile mind root—like a tree
While the rain surrounds my comfort
And seduces me to sleep

Cave

Things haven't been the same
since my boy screwed me figuratively
and my girl kicked me literally—
out of her life

and as bad as that is
I know some folks
and have seen others who have it worse
but somehow,
that don't make me feel any better
I'd rather think about anything else
but my analyst, ok my shrink
keeps wanting me to think
think about my past
rehash this trash
cause that's the only way to get beyond
this place

this cynical place I've come to
a place where days are spent in caves
while the world goes spinning by
oblivious to me and me to it
everything is dark
and without purpose
there's no spark to inspire
any-work towards anything for anyone
when in the end,
this cave is all I have to retire my thoughts to

III. That's Life

...in a world where X's and O's eventually end in W's or L's.

Dreams

sitting here thinking about
whens and what ifs
my pulse quickens
on thoughts of time spent
I sigh,
smiling…content
as wonders of nights fly by
and dreams of days
turn quietly in my head

pictures of warm breezes
lazy Sundays and papers
spread across my bed
all float through my mind
overpowering thoughts of
lies and denies
that spoiled earlier lives
'cause the very thing we look for
finds us
the very minute we stop looking
the very instant we stop pressing
and stressing ourselves out

who knows better
of "what could bes"
than the man who
dares to live his dreams?
to fly high and soar
while others snore
then complain that
opportunity and life
have passed them by

Checking Out

Day and night are the people
who show their souls
or hide them through
their shut off life
each pull of the tide tugs at the insider
struggling to escape the walls of earthly plains
that have yielded nothing but pain
so this must be hell

What a difference a day makes
as you yell ticket please
looking to check out quietly
while a spirit inside
fights to hold on to
a belief, hoping for that miracle
that's been saved for relief

Fools no doubt,
have died for more glorious pursuits
be they socially or civic-ly redeemable
death remains a watcher at the wheel
ready to collect his lot
each time the roulette marble stops
it's all the same in the end
it's grim
as you watch that marble ball
tick and bounce
waiting for it to stop
facing yourself across the wheel
all but dead on the outside
and ½ way there on the inside

Fatal Thoughts

My finger is paused
on the pulse of time
ready to caress the trigger
ready to make time stand still…
I figure,
when it's time to go
my will be done
and
I'm not going alone.
In finality you'll know
my frailties, my differences,
and my weaknesses
protected you, not me
shielded you
from the strength of fatal thoughts
from the statistic,
the example you are dying to be.

My finality is lifeless
unable to move the straw
covering broken camels' backs
representing the totality of
verbal and physical attacks,
of everything endured
when things could have been
as they should have been
like matinee movies
with happy endings
or like I hoped, wished
or wanted them to be.

But no one hears a kid like me
no one sees me cry,
no one saw me break,
no one heard my scream
I CAN'T TAKE IT ANYMORE...
I WON'T TAKE IT ANYMORE!

In the end,
no one saw my fatal thoughts,
no one was a friend.

I Am

Part I

I'm a young boy watching tv. I see a coffin being pulled on a cart, the coffin is covered with an American flag. I am very young, but can I sense the tension in the room, something is wrong. They tell me he was a good president. I am too young to know.

I watch cartoons and read comic books. I am GI Joe with the Kung Fu grip. I have to have my PF flyers, how else can I run faster and jump higher? Everybody else has them. I get up at the crack of dawn on Christmas morning. I am a child

I am, Somebody! A man is marching with more people than I have ever seen before. "I have a dream!", he said and something else, something about getting to the promised land. If he was so good for everyone, why was he killed for his dream? If he preached non-violence, why are people fighting? I've seen the TV change from black and white to color, and I guess America forgot to change with it. Burn baby Burn, by any means necessary…Why? I am confused.

I am growing. Where do I fit in? Blacks don't believe, Whites aren't sure, and the scholars don't have time to care. Where are all the guidance counselors? Dad, can I have the keys to the car? Ma, I really need gas money. How else will I get to Coney Island after the Prom? I blink and I'm graduating. What am I going to do with my life? It doesn't matter, I know everything! I'm invincible! I'm a teenager.

Time and life passes…I grow, I am a college student, I am an adult, I am a worker, I am a man!

I drive across this country. The salt-flats of Utah, the Grand Canyon, the snowcapped Teton Mountains and the flat farmlands of Iowa and Nebraska full of corn and cows. So this is America? Funny, it doesn't look the great melting pot. I am a traveler.

Part II

I'm traveling on the road of life…somewhere between I don't know and I don't care. Born between the boom and gen-x'ers and just who are the dot com-ers? Who am I?
I am a child of the media, the images, the environment
of cold wars and global warming
of upstarts and downsizing
of sit-ins and walk-outs
of agent-orange and desert storms
of a European mess and a stained blue dress
of Watergate cover-ups, and Rodney King beat-downs
of a man on the moon and the World Trade Center's BOOM!
of MTV, 24 hour sports and all the news all the time…at 6, I mean 5, I mean tonight at 11 or; Is it 10 o'clock? By the way, do you know where your children are?

I am everything that's fit to print; and many things that aren't…imbedded in my brain.
I think, therefore I am!   I think, therefore I can.
i am   I am   I AM!

Tarnished

Up from black...
Lights—camera—action
Cinematic dreams scream
with climatic scenes
as villains toil, upstage and block
to foil the roles we play
on life's journey

While working and refining crafts
searching the roles
for the outstanding part
portraying characters in
the perfect performance
overwhelming audience
approval sealed with
thunderous applause
leaving ovations standing
as bravo's echo innumerable curtain calls
bows before the final curtain falls

Fade to black
in the last city
on the last day
of the final tour
There, in the black
backstage of your mind
with vanity spots
shining through
rose covered three sided mirrors

That's Life

make up smears on cold creamed tissues
as the character is wiped away
the perfect part
now but an empty stage
just as the fading memories of lines and actions
tarnished but kept alive
by saved tattered reviews

Hustle

Hustling to keep up with the Joneses
who bustle through everyday life
while I feel like a
hitchhiker with a sore thumb.

I spin in concentric circles
till the room turns oblong and pops.
It bursts at the seams like vertigo,
I mean Virgo—er go—
I chase the virgin fair maiden,
per chance to dream.

For she can stop my spinning
with her pure touch of innocence
this insolence must stop
before I too pop
and silence
will be the only sound I utter
as did the raven, nevermore.

No more "Rosebud" or
et tu Brute?
and I won't be good
till the last drop
when my last drop
has been given
in a fight not worth winning
so shhhhhh
while I quietly step away.

A-D-D

Hands raise high
when questions fly
screams of glee
and smiles so wide
look to give the answer
one more time

But I sit back
staring out of windows
and counting cracks
no one cares about me
I'm the one with A-D-D.

Hands raise high
as my steel shines bright
to all you fools
so damn smart in school

I take what you have
'cause I just don't care
remembering that no one cared
I'm the one with A-D-D.

Still Splitting

Standing in the face of smiles
judging looks, hair and dress
whispers in the back
cutting deeper than knives
sharpened by the lies
behind those smiles
still splitting US
so we don't stay in one place too long
gotta move up, gotta move on

What happened to smiles
that reached helping hands
each one teaching one
might I lend you a hand?
power and purpose
destinations in sight
pushing through struggles
supporting what's right

Urban flight for the have-s
let's forget THOSE have-nots
no more neighbors
looking after the block
it's now just the folks next door
and their doors are all locked
unlisted numbers, barely a nod or a wave
just a bunch of people divided
divided like slaves
so don't even bother to ask for
sugar, milk, or an egg

Remembering history now dormant
it's getting harder to see
they didn't make BP II or III
(Black Power sequels)
seems the 2nd month each year
don't have much play on MTV or BET
the "Thomas Principle" is now our pal
it's the mating call of the boo-shwa-z
I worked for mine, THEY can get theirs
and; I still ain't getting involved

Their work is done
no more neighborhoods with
neighbors as close as family
neighborhoods with our doctors and dentists
with our shopkeepers and tailors
no more teachers or mentors
no more tradesmen or their apprentices

Assimilation
complements in the highest sense
proper English by day,
but when the fellas are around,
hacking verbs and past tense
wouldn't want to be perceived as soft
and all that would be cool
if we'd think about the past and the future,
in the gated communities…just reflect on the struggle
just think for even this minute
'cause there is still a struggle
and we still caught up in it

Tainted Glasses

Clouds roll in and storm my mind
and blind my sight…
and I can't see no silver lining
because my world has been tainted
with rose colored glasses
I see the refuse
blowing through the wind
hanging around like
pieces of paper
stuck on a fence
or on some city street corner
profiling and styling
mouth always running
while brain is on idle
from puffing or snorting,
or dropping some cycles
stoned always there
like the old cigar statue

Hearin' them bitchin' bout their
40 acres and a mule
but the only action they take is
hat passing
collecting some cash
for a 40 with a Bull.
and I pass on by covered
by the shadows of clouds
that storm in my mind and
blind my sight
my world, you see,

has been tainted
with rose colored glasses

I walk, arms up and ready
as the pungent odors of alleys
and molding unopened cellars
ooze like dead spirits from
black asphalt and rusting grates
graying cracked concrete,
high-rise red bricks,
boarded brownstones
and windows locked with gates

Am I locked out or,
is it you who's locked in?
locked in this circle
of gloom and doom
while rhetorically screaming
ya got things to take care of
but…the man's got you down
yet you won't stand up
on your own
just keep hanging round
spending money and
losing time
borrowing on tomorrows
becoming a fixture while the weight of yesterdays
compress your world into never
ending todays

I need a condom
a rubber,

a latex piece of protection
to sheath me from
the grit and grime and slime
of the city
where moving on up
is epitomized by
leaving your one bedroom apartment on the 4th floor
for a two bedroom apartment on the 12th
even though
the elevators rarely work
and you still can't get a pizza
or Chinese food delivered
just so all your kids will have 1 room

Put me in the bag and
twist the tie at the bottom
cover me so
I no longer have to see
the shadows of clouds that
storm my mind and
blind my sight
let me sleep
so I won't have to look through
these tainted rose colored glasses

Lioness

When you walked across the room, your body moved like molten lava working its oozing magic down towards the relief of a cooling ocean. A hot flowing magnet in search of a cooling force. Heads turned and followed you around, you knew it and you loved it. No one dared get in your way for fear of instant disintegration. You had attitude and purpose to your movement and nothing could stop you from the man you wanted. Any man you wanted!

Looking into your eyes one could see the darkness of a stormy day. A gray black sky that dares birds to fly. That lifelessness served as a warning flag—waving in the wind, but like the thrill walking through a hurricane men would stand in line ignoring the warning in hopes of getting closer to you.

You sized up your play ground the way a lioness sizes her domain. You picked your target for the night. He had been standing at the bar, alone as best as you could tell. You immediately took note of your challenge running your game through your mind, how you would quickly find his weakness and bring him down to his knees. "Probably one of those players!", you thought to yourself as you fought back the surly curl of your upper lip. They were the only men challenging enough now days. You had worked your way through the shy, humble, do anything for you men…and taken them for everything they had. Whatever you wanted, they gave under your spell. And as quickly as you used them up, you threw them away. Your bedpost was notched with many a victory. But they no longer challenged you. You now craved bigger prey. You were ready to put the trophy in your room. Your lust could only be satisfied by bringing down the beast, the king of the night-time jungle.

You knew your movements blew men away and you controlled every move you made. Slow and seductive; you moved your hot magma towards him. He was immediately overtaken with your beauty and aggressiveness, and more than happy to get you a drink, several drinks. He laughed at your jokes and put his best gentleman show on for you. His mama taught him well. You had him moving on the floor all night, and felt your ultimate power when you made him fetch your coat for you. All the while he just smiled. He was being worked, and he had no idea. He just smiled…the unknowing smile of an animal on his way to slaughter. This beast would be yours tonight!

He drove you home. All the way, you were throwing him compliments and melting him down. You were going to make him squirm and crawl and be your puppy dog. You knew you'd be a winner tonight; everything was just as you dreamed.

Your place was immaculate. You put your hands in his and asked him to light the candles, so you could slip into something more comfortable. You called out and asked him to make a couple of drinks. When you appeared you slyly took note that his jaw dropped open.

You sipped drinks and made small talk, you had the beast in your hands, putty…this was going to be a trophy to remember! The lioness was about to go in for the kill.

You jumped up in your bed when the sun came into your window and realized you were alone. You shook your head trying to clear the cobwebs. You had never felt this way before, never had a hangover before and yet you were dazed and confused. It wasn't until you got out of bed until you realized you were completely undressed. You walked over to your closet to get your robe still trying to put together what happened. When you open your closet, you jaw dropped! Empty, no robe, no clothes, no nothing.

You checked your dresser; all the drawers were empty. Even your dirty clothes hamper…empty. You ran into the other rooms…empty, all of your art, your jewelry, your tv and stereo, even the food in the fridge,…gone. Everything, gone!

You rushed to call the police, determined that he wasn't going to get away with this! You ran about frantically looking for your phone. Then you realized, your phones were gone too. You stood there, naked, confused, and wondering. It was then you spotted roses on your dining room table. Under the arrangement there were a dozen Polaroids. Pictures of you with many of the very men you had used. There was a card in the flowers.

"From my Brothers and Me, thanks for a unforgettable night of pleasure, you're the best! Call us anytime." It was signed…King of the Jungle.

Phone Don't Ring

When the phone don't ring
There is nothing but time
You pick up and make sure there's a tone

When the phone don't ring
You question just why,
as you dig deeper and deeper inside

When the phone don't ring
The silence is loud
So loud, you can't hear yourself think

When the phone don't ring
You're all alone
It's time to learn just who you are

My phone don't ring when I want it to.
I've been patient and more than fair.
I inspect that lifeless plastic life-line
to make sure it's hung up
to make sure that thin wire is snapped into the box.
I even picked up that face-hugging box
and listen for that low toned buzz
just to make sure it's set and ready to ring.

Around my room, there's nothing but time,
Quiet time
I get to know myself better than I want to
probably better than I should.
I face the demon—that demon that waits to catch you

in the silent moments of your life
That demon—you know the one, who never—ever stops
    talking;
talking about the what ifs, the should have dones,
and the could have beens......
All because that phone don't ring.

I'm getting tired of waiting for that stupid phone to ring
Tired of making excuses for it
And tired of talking to myself

It's like a child responding after every answer
Why?...
Only the wise know why
Thus...the question remains...why?
All because, the phone don't ring?

Chase You Down

Chasing you down, waving my arms
like I left my bag in a taxi that
just pulled away.
Am I a madman or a psycho? No!
I'm just chasing after you
like a man who just missed his bus
and can't afford to be late to work, again.

It may appear
that I'm some sort of nut
but I'm no pervert,
and to revert back to the story,
I only saw you once.
Uncertain that I would ever see you again,
my heart and mind danced and soared
35,000 thousand feet
spinning above the sanity and calm
of the clouds below
fantasizing of fantasies
till my destination became a reality

There was no space or place
for me to speak or us to meet.
Just trapped in my spot
by uncaring captors
I wished time would stop
to escape my distracters
for only a moment and
allow my attraction
a moment with you

for a minute of seconds
to hear your voice focused
in my direction.

Please listen...I don't mean you any harm
there's really no cause for alarm
I was just so overwhelmed
perhaps even—hypnotically charmed
like the slow climb to the top of the roller coaster incline
seeming like a good idea at the time
until the drop!
But I knew I had to chase you down.

I'm Glad You Called

I'm glad you called
Been waiting
Waiting anxiously
Watching the phone
And waiting
Turning in my bed
Tossing under my cover
Waiting, for your call

Reverberating rings
Echoes off walls
Igniting a powder-keg of emotion
A rush of excitement
A special connection
That removes the need
for explanations
dropping our most
secure defenses
knowing who we are
knowing what we like

Behind the security
of my comforter
And the solitude
of closed eyelids
I see your face
And fantasize
Your smile, your skin

Like a teenager,
I'm giddy

I'm tingly
all over
Wishing your words were
touching me directly
from your lips
to my ears
From my lips
to your body
From my heart
To your soul

Non stop giggling
shared feelings
Ticklish without being touched
Magic!
Talking 'bout nothing
Talking 'bout everything
Magic!
I feel you
you feel me
I'm glad you called

Searching

Flash bulbs pop and strobe lights blink
matching heart beats and dancing eyelids.
White dots chase in convexed retinas
blinding the way from here.

Amber street lights and hazards
paint caution golden on the corner
where disappointment meets disgust,
and the fork ahead
leads down the road to despair.
Red eyes stop to look for answers
entranced by the hypnotic blinking glow.

Fingers snap judgments that
carry thoughts and dreams
down a salty sea of tears
while this vessel
sets sail for a distant port
and a solid shore.

Lying

I can't stop lying
it is easier to lie
than live in my truth
the reality is that truth hurts
and as long as I lie to myself
and to others
I don't have to feel that pain
my super-imposed reality
is a world of characters
that I've created and control
and though they don't pray to me
I am their god!

Lies—lives and deaths
Standing attention to respect
the emotion flowing through
my fingertips
with detail that organizes
homage and reverence into
"I'm OK, You're OK", books
so I can continue
on that "Road Less Traveled"
so my characters
are positioned to help me deal
their prophecy,
to complete me
or take the chance of facing me
face to face
fearing the fate of the backspace
or even worse
the complete
highlighted delete!

Dark Corners

Spring cleaning long since past;
old articles collect again and again
in the attic and dark corners
of damp cellar walls.
Goods—long past their usefulness
serve as anchor points for spider webs
while dust settles quietly like snowflakes
and silver linings begin to tarnish.

Tick-tock fall leaves
down on rocks
like mountain snow
cascading in an avalanche
and once the passion
begins to fail
everything in its way
falls with it.
There's no stopping
till hitting rock bottom.

Dust balls and cob-webs gather
while waiting
and waiting for the next Spring
to have reason to clean.
This thing is too clouded.
The window to the soul is hazed
hiding behind dark drapes and shades.
It's no longer clear and I fear,
spring will never get here.

That's Life

Tick-tock sweeps the second hand
brushing and collecting every minute
in the attic and damp cellar walls.
Collected, piled and stored in stacks
of dark corners
called the past.

Love's Thug

Cupid appeared silently through the cool night air in-
 between starlight and moon-beams
His wings flapped like a moth, wings looking too little to
 carry his weight
but he flew nonetheless; searching, prowling, spying eyes
 wide like an owl
looking along the street for a couple so he could start fresh
 romance
ready to ignite the burn of attraction that feeds the heat and
 consumes the couple's heart at the start

In the distance, a woman and a man walked along—about to
 pass one another
Cupid set his arrows, locked his sights and fired
arrows sped through the night and met their marks with a
 light prick
Just the wisp of a web or a thread, those invisible strands you
 feel but never see
just a flick, to make them look into each another's eyes
the look was enough to start them off slow and allow things
 to build
Cupid did not want to burn them in lust like an unchecked
 wick

Their eyes locked at first sight. Compelled to speak within
 this instant
smiles curled up and defenses took flight
traded numbers, yet kept the conversation light

each secretly thinking, "what the hell?"
while Cupid sat back in the shadows struggling to contain his
    delight

Their dates were filled with laughter and late night talks on
    the phone
conversations mixed with giggles and whispers of fantasies
Cupid kept tabs and waited to get in the game
for the moment to play, he waited to send love's arrows to slay
    them
to give thoughts of love, lust and rolls in the hay
to play them with blissful wishes and honey drenched kisses
so they would venture into love and the fierce tranquility of
    making love

One night after dinner and drinks they felt a combined tingle
she had been getting hot for him, ran her toes up his shins—
    he grinned
this platonic friendship no longer a whim, she was hot and
    hungry for him,
ready to dive headfirst into cooling pleasure and swim
through the depths of destined fantasies to come true for them

Cupid watched and conspired, followed them to her place to
    set them on fire,
to brand love deep inside their hearts, his arrows ready to
    ignite their desire
and heat up their passions so their actions would be the foun-
    dation, for love's lustful attraction

That's It!

Cupid reached back, grabbed an arrow from its sling
set his aim, ready to do his thing, Cupid was so focused on
    hitting the ring
That he never saw Love's Thug rolling up on him—"Ding!"

Love's Thug had been laying waiting to play too,
he had been just behind the scenes with his too big shirt and
    oversized jeans
and when Cupid wasn't looking, he got beat
surprised by Thug and hit, blind-sided—Thug went on his
    noggin,
"take that for love, sucker!" Then he took out a rope and tied
    him,
left him outside, so he could undo what Cupid was starting

Thug ran inside, found them in the den
he had to work quick to kill this love mix
they had begun getting all hot and steaming
buttons undone he could hear heavy breathing
heating up with hands roaming and lips gleaming
goo goo eyes and coos
and parts of bodies begging for touch and relief
and that stupid lovers' talk, all soft and low
filled with wet kisses on necks and soft bites on ear lobes
their bodies burning, flaming like a bonfire
all cuddled up, hugging, playing footsy, and smiling

Unseen and unheard in the heated mayhem
Thug crushed their foreplay unbeknownst to them
within the blink of an eye he grabbed her insides
took her warm heart and started, spinning and digging
upside down, inside out—pulling, stomping and kicking

Thug's dark aura had locked on her heart
It grabbed her and stoned her which cooled them apart
In that split second—her mood changed, she went from
    burning hot to cold
her body rigid, she pushed away from his hold
her warm eyes, now ice, took on a blank stare
Thug froze her over, what was she doing there?

Never saw it coming, couldn't possibly understand,
Thug's drive-by was indefensible, totally insensible
they looked at each other dumbfounded, surprised.
    Incomprehensible.
her man all worked up, lathered, salivating with thoughts of
    tasting her essence,
his mind fore-telling premonitions of pleasure
freedom, at last, the inevitable release of souls held in captivity
within the desert of his loins for far too long
finally ready to fulfill both of their fantasies
ready—longing—begging to know her, ready to let his people
    go

That very instant he reached to her and pulled her tight
unknowingly—unwittingly—unexpectedly he received the
    most hated phrase heard during
the crucial time of impending pardoned prisoner release…
"No, not tonight—I'm not in the mood", how rude,
it was as if she had dropped a cleaver, severing things, her soul
    was on ice

Never would they realize what happened that night, only the
    empty feel of love taking flight away from their hearts, in
    that split second between combustible consummation
    and consternation

they were left as dazed and confused as Cupid—still tied up
     outside
Love's Thug found it hard to contain himself as he chuckled,
he stomped out ecstasy, solidifying this as their last date
he had turned them away never to become lovers, their fate to
     remain just insignificant others
and with that comforting thought,
Love's Thug silently disappeared through the cool night air
     in-between starlight and moon-beams

IV. Questionable Optimism

Are you making me
wait for you?
Is this the game
I play for you;
by counting calls
as messages fall
down the notepad path
of so what?

In My Dreams

i saw you once upon a time
in a dream where roses grew
and since dreams are only in my mind
i gave up on ever finding you…

you're a composite of infatuations
how could i ever expect to find you?
just a bunch of wishes from imaginations
and MY dreams have never come true

can this dream be real for me?
there's a warmth, a touch, i know it's you
i want that dream so much inside
i dreamed i woke up, and i saw you!

Big Dipper

The big dipper reached across the sky,
grabbed a bucket full of stars
and poured me a bowl full of hope

It was as though this
cosmic fly-through-waitress
knew exactly what I needed

Didn't give me any of those false promises
I usually get stuck paying for
when the bill comes

Just a big bowl of hope
poured over red clay
in between mountain tops
at my feet

And I think I heard her say
"be careful, this is hot!…
if you eat it too soon,
or too fast, you'll get burned"

I thanked the big dipper
for giving me just what I needed,
a bowl of hope and
a drop of cosmic understanding,
that while wants are fleeting
patience will allow me to enjoy
every sincere hope in time

Jump In

I stand on the ledge with my toes gripping tightly, secure on the slippery ground. I hold my head high and arch my back to make sure I fall away from the unknown. I've taken this plunge many times before and if you know as well as I, the water is very cold when you first jump in.

My confidence is tested. A breeze blows by. I'm suddenly reminded of my openness to everyone around, even those who don't know me! I sense they can see me, maybe even see through me. Time is slowing to a stop, waiting for me to jump. I hesitate as I think…the water is mostly cold when you first jump in.

My stomach feels empty. I can suddenly hear my heart beat. My mouth has gone dry and my body tingles. I feel each goose bump rise in anticipation of the leap. My mind races and I shiver with thoughts of the plunge and my teeth begin to chatter. After all, the water is usually cold when you first jump in.

The verbal sparring and interrogation begins; me at you and you at me. Learning the who, what, when, where, and why-s. We give and we get what we think we need to know…and for now it makes the hunt challenging. Maybe, challenging enough to continue; if you can stand it. The water *is* sometimes cold when you first jump in.

Even the man who knows not fully himself, knows the full truth lies somewhere between here—this ledge, and the bottom of the unknown. Some never reach their goal because, "*they're so sure*", they know how the water is when you first jump in. But if you never jump you'll never realize the truth…Most of the truth that is, the water is only cold when you first jump in…and it's not so bad after that!

Morning —Another Day

Moonset tugs
on fog melting into mist
while tiny particles
grasp to cling as dew

On the center
of a blade of grass
they congregate like
Sunday morning service
into one mighty drop

The blade bends
to cushion the clear tear drop's
leap of faith to earth
to work its way down to the root
as if the grass were tipping
a glass of refreshment

Melting gray mist
lifts like a comforter in the pale light
yielding hues of green, brown, and blue
while purple and yellow wild flowers
cover landscape views
like bed sheets stretching to meet the sky

Stars, one by one, dim out their lights
so the sun can proudly beam
on this, another day

Miss Tick

Through a door and past dark curtains, opium thick heavy incense, candle light and hanging beads, one would weave their way away from the noise, concrete and bricks of the heartless city into a marvelously mystical and magical dream world, the world of Miss Tick.

Miss Tick was a magical mystic. Her mystique was captivating and her charm was magical. Magical Miss Tick would spin tales with her mind's eye and tell the fortunes and misfortunes for the many people who stopped into her den of dreams.

There, there were large velvet chairs that would engulf you as you sat. Chairs that would welcome you in their arms like your distant aunt. The one who was always happy to see you, the one who demanded and took kisses, hugged you in her healthy bosom, pinched your cheeks and then told you how much you'd grown. Chairs that would take the pressure away, relax your body, and allow you to float on a magical carpet ride.

Mystical Miss Tick would look through the dark smoky haze in the room. Look directly in your eyes and ask, "Do you believe? The magic of the mystic can only work for believers." Once confirmed, Miss Tick would go into a trance-like state and begin to tell of things for the mindful. She would tell of things that had been, and of things to come and that monetary wishes could only lead to myopic minds, *and that* would not help in making life any easier. That heartache and pain were but momentary yet necessary mountains to get to one's meaningful existence. Like Zen's Yin and Yang, one could not exist without the other and still keep harmony and balance. The best of the best would never be appreciated without feeling the worst of the worst.

But the true magic came when Miss Tick spoke of overcoming the pain. She said that the pain was momentary, and in the course of a meaningful life it was largely inconsequential. Miraculously, every time a mountain was scaled, newly found meanings would be discovered. While the mountains might appear high from the bottom, the top would disclose a new horizon to look beyond. One would recognize what was overcome, and realize that those once mighty mountains were nothing more than molehills in our ever expanding open minded memory, making our existence much more meaningful.

Many would begin their meetings with Miss Tick believing it's a mistake to see a mystic. But after meeting the magnificent mystic, Miss Tick, they leave mysteriously moved, their faith in themselves magnified a million-fold. They feel magnificently alive, and that is marvelously magical!

What Happened to My Music?

What happened to my music?
I lived, I loved and I laughed
The world was right; it had to be
There was always a melody or a lyrical muse to make things all right
>"BABY EVERYTHING'S ALRIGHT, UPTIGHT, CLEAR OUT
>OF SIGHT!"

It was coming from my radio/cassette/8-track
and it was in my head
I was moved, I was creative, and I was happy

What happened to my music?
I knew all the words, and I could twist, I could jerk, I could hustle and I could slooooow jam!
Cinder block walls perspiring from the heat of the night yet cool to the touch
Blue Lights in the Basement was my invitation to work it out, "WE CAN WORK IT OUT"
Motown, Salsoul, The Sound of Philadelphia, EARTH WIND AND FIRE!
Music blended and bonded us all together…OHH YEAH……SAY YEAHH

What happened to my music?
"AIN'T TOO PROUD TO BEG, SWEET DARLIN"
It was my thing, my focus, it was me, it was my life
No tears, no heartache, nothing could pierce my musical armor
"CAUSE BEAUTY'S ONLY SKIN DEEP…OOOOH YEAH!"
I was wide open, I was loving and I was giving
"IF THIS WORLD WERE MINE, I WOULD PLACE AT YOUR FEET

ALL THAT I OWN, YOU'VE BEEN SO GOOD TO ME
IF THIS WORLD WERE MINE."

What happened to my music?
It was just right here…here in my hands. I was holding it and it had me.
It consumed me.
"PAPA WAS A ROLLING STONE" and this is a "HARD KNOCK
LIFE"
It's all a "BALL OF CONFUSION…THAT'S WHAT THE WORLD IS
TODAY"
It's electro, it's techno, or is it hip-pop or rock—hop?
I can't keep up with the Joneses…I don't even know who the Joneses are
anymore
I've lost control, I've lost my mind, I've lost my music…

What happened to my music?

Brother, Brother

Brother, Brother
I see you looking at me
Up and down
Wondering about me and who I am
You give me a nod, barely an acknowledgement
You don't even bother to say hello
I am not your competition

Brother, Brother
I see you round the way
Marking your territory
Holding your woman
Making sure all who walk by
Knows what's up
I am not your competition

Brother, Brother
I see you in the club
I know that's your space
I see those are your friends
I guess you are the man
I am not your competition

Brother, Brother
I see you in need
When the money is gone
The women are gone
Your so-called friends are gone
But, I am still here
Here to listen to you

To support you
To help you stand
To see you grow!

Brother, Brother
You see,
I am not your competition
I am your Brother

Castle King

I dreamed of one day being…At least I thought I would…
Be a King and rule greatly my land
The King of my castle and reign regally.
You know, the family figure-head with a coat-of-arms, shield
and all.

I had a Queen of Hearts…or so I thought
A Queen who would compliment the plans for our Kingdom
One who would stand by the Kingdom through thick and thin
And help fend off feudal uprisings

Each weekday the King would venture to the remote nether-
lands to slay the work dragon;
There he wielded absolute power, unless he got a memo
directive from his manager
There the King would collect fees due him, and he would con-
tinue his ascension up the tree like ladder of corporate
America
Trees that pointed to the sky and invited the bravest to the
thin limbs at the top
Where only the few—true lords dared dream of climbing
And he attended parties for social subliming.

But things quickly changed in the Kingdom un-magical.
The King soon discovered that his Queen was a radical
The Queen of Hearts was actually the Queen of Spades in
disguise.
The King was crushed. Damn, what a surprise!

The Queen of Spades had been on a quest herself, searching
    for the King's diamonds.
Once she secured the diamonds, the disguise was lifted and
    the King found himself but a figure head on the throne
    without the power to rule.
He had no power and found himself a subject, a mere slave
To the incessant nagging and the Queen's tirades.

He was nothing more than the moat keeper
The cinder sweeper
The shhhh; be quiet, you better not make a peep-er
The pupil of the do as I say—not as I do teacher
Full of "Yes Dear!" answers
To love's grim reaper

No matter what he did, the Queen found fault. She was just a
    taker, as it all turned out,
For once the King's diamonds were gone, he no longer had
    clout.
She nit-picked his ability as a dragon slayer
For not finding the trees; for not cleaning the lair,
She criticized, nagged him, and needled him to death
She told him to leave, he finally left.

Now the castle is lonely, it's cold, dark, and plain
It's the Queen of Spade's domicile forever to reign;
But a diamond can never be produced there again…
A diamond needs years to develop, it's only coal it's merely
    earth rock
That rock needs the warmth of the King and the heat of a heart!

Desert Pallet

Clouds came to life
as the sun was setting
starting as white
and changing
to red; to orange; to purple
foreshadowing
every shade of a blue sky

They framed brown-black mountains
in every direction
pale green trees and bushes
were surrounded by
sandy brown earth

The moon glowed white
as stars appeared above,
one by one
twinkling every color in the spectrum
like mixtures of dollops of paint
on an artist's pallet

Love's Illusion

Is it moist...
Is it moist...
Is it moist on your lips
as you prepare for a kiss?
when you close you eyes
do you get all warm inside?
as excitement drips from the tips
of every nerve in your body
at the instant when space is displaced
by time and never wanting
that moment to end
but it does

Have you come
Have you come
Have you come to the conclusion
that love's just an illusion
that taunts and baits
and makes your heart wait
while your mind plays tricks
and your stomach feels sick
till you look like you feel
questioning, "Is this for real?"

Searching for attraction
that quickly turns to lust
and you grope and you thrust
'cause know you must
get something off your head tonight

be it wrong or right
you move it along
till it comes
till it comes
till you come
and you both sigh
goodnight.

Moon and Star

The moon was followed
across the sky
by one star

Everywhere
the moon went
that one star followed

From right to left
across the sky
the star was there by her side

From horizon to horizon
the star followed
catching traces of moon dust
and wished he could be closer

My Brown Girl

My Brown Girl
has long brown hair
Or short, with curls,
sometimes locked
She's tall and lean,
eyes sparkle and gleam
And her look gets me
excited and hot

Strong enough
to raise me up
the tenderness
to lay me back down
Her voice; so calm,
it soothes, never harsh
It's a smile she can make
from my frown

My Brown Girl
has soft, smooth hands
She holds me
close and safe in her arms
I'm comforted by
her silk, satin strokes
When her fingers dance
I am charmed

She has the mind
of genius and scholar
But can act the fool
just for me

She knows what to say
or when just to listen
the ability
to keep me at peace

My Brown Girl
Will always love me
Some say
she's too good to be true
She's always there
When ever I need
and she loves me
through and through

You see My Brown Girl
Is too good to be true
She is here
here only for me
She accepts me fully
Doesn't need me to change
She's in my mind-
And she loves me unconditionally

Valentine

Will you be my Valentine?
Will you be there all the time?
In the darkness, when the sun don't shine?
Or will I just see rain?

Will you tell me soft sweet things?
Or make me jump through hoops and rings?
Will I be your everything?
Or will I just feel pain?

Will you take the hurt away?
On those cold and gloomy days?
Tell me that you're here to stay
Ain't playin' no more games

Let me keep you by my side
and fight the foes in life's long ride
keep you warm and safe inside
No rain, no hurt, no fear!

I want to hold you, close like this
When we're together I feel life's bliss
Come close to me for one more kiss
Don't let me die again!

Desert Tear

Mountain peaks rise
behind ridges of rocks
above rivers that carry
the silt of being that forms
the ends of the earth

Sands unlock life in muddy banks
while willows weep
sway and sachet
like long arms waving goodbye

The desert keeps life locked
in dry river beds
its rivers long been cried out
red eyes sunrise
toil for one more tear of life

The Big Game

ATM receipts flow from my hand
like a mini ticker tape parade
I create a paper trail as I
search like a magician
in his big black hat of tricks
to find my last cash
that emergency stash
usually for gas
that's past my
blood donor card,
behind my license and photos
under the secret flap in my wallet
I scream, "Eureka, I have found it!"
as I pull my last prayer
in God we trust,
for the BIG GAME

I've been praying on this
I can feel it's my lot
'cause I'm in too deep to quit
this is the BIG GAME
ain't no little stuff
like c-lo, sidewalk craps
or Atlantic City slots that never spit
money back my way
or them damn nag horses
looking good in the stalls
that never show in the money for me

Gonna let the machine
pick my picks

I can feel it, I'm gonna hit
and won't have to worry about
this old car and this old job
they can both kiss my ass
and all of you who
think you know better
always try'n to tell me something
I'm gonna save a spot just for you too
'cause it's my time
it's the BIG GAME

Oh the Big Game
has to call my name
it's the third time I've played
in the past two weeks
and the only reason
I didn't win then
is because God must want to make sure
I get the big pot…right?
for all those times I tithed…
well, gave what I could
well ok, I gave a dollar or two

I can go without hanging out,
wait for that drink 'til payday, and
if I only drive from home to work
and back home
I won't need no gas anyway
and tomorrow it won't matter
cause by then I'll be a winner
cause I'm in the BIG GAME

V. Mostly Truth

i can only change right now
while memories of the past go by
and thoughts cross roads into forks
i curl into the spoon position
and lament on decisions
that pass into history
and the revelation that
yesterday will never change

Sunset

Knowing the sun will set soon
I think about all of the sunsets
we have shared
at different times
in different places
watching the same sun
warm our face from different spaces
unifying strangely this common force
reminding us we are only apart in body
and never apart in spirit

This day, like tomorrow un-promised
has been given for at-least this moment
alive today and living
and with this in mind
hopefully living to the fullest
for we are connected by this experience
that bids farewell to the day
and welcomes the night
on a radiating carpet of golden warmth
the opportunity comes to decide
what to do next
as we pray for just that chance

We have this—this day
while waves break on sandy shores
when dark clouds part after the storm
while watching endless blue skies
and jet stream trails

by stopping and pulling over to look
and just taking the minute to watch
rays radiating
watching the same sun set
as I think to myself
you can feel it too!

Universal Mother

Mother, our earth—
wraps us in her arms
as we travel through
this galaxy called life
fearless in the face
of unknown and darkness;
bringing joy, easing pain,
hugging away hurt
and comforting our way
through life

Mother, our foundation
plants us in
soil of brown
next to
clear seas of blue
seasons and lessons
provide life's forces
that nurture us through
and into our nature
as we ripen and mature
into colorful flowers and gems

Mother, our teacher
her hands
sturdy like the mighty oak
holds steady
and keeps us on course
her voice, calm and soothing
like the breeze
sings songs of history

sings songs of truth
sings songs of hope
sings songs of praise

Mother, our future
sees deep
within our hearts
without judging
errant ways
understanding life
is for living
and shows us

Mother, our earth
takes her place
just past starlight
revolving around the sun
in praise of
our heavenly father
Bless you!
Mother

Ode to Chris

Chris was from a family probably a-lot just like yours
He studied at school and at night he did chores
He knew how to live, he partied, and had fun
All day he worked hard but at night he would run
Run to the clubs, to the bars and the blocks
To find those brothers with beepers, from whom he could cop

A bag for a nickel, a dime sometimes two
And disappear in the smoke, to get his head new
Chris would drink and smoke to get his head tight
He soon too discovered that the powder was nice
He did his dirt, some booze, coke and weed
But as he continued, he began more to need

He found a crew with whom he could swing
Guys just like him getting high was the thing
Chris was hanging with obviously the wrong crew
He stopped working and studying, and just looked for new—
Ways to get high, all day and all night
No eating, no sleeping, just a head getting tight

Chris was no longer just a casual user
He fiended and needed, he became an abuser
He used and abused and became not himself
He ran out of money so he took others' wealth
Just to keep getting high he even tried crime
But the cops caught up with him and the judge gave him time

Chris did his time, paid society's dues
He cleaned himself out no longer to use
He got out of there and went straight to NA

"I'm Chris, I abused", very humbly he'd say,
"I could have been dead, thank God I'm alive,
"I'll do all I can to help others survive"

Chris found himself a healthy free man
Born again, second chance, he developed a plan
To pick his-self up and make himself proud
To shake other men, if he had to yell loud
As a living example, showing how he overcame
And they could do it too, without any shame

Chris climbed up far from down that drug block
He's motivated and determined to scale each mountain top
By staying clean he got his degree and also a Masters
He's now a counselor saving others from disaster
The need-ers and users see a friend in his face
He supports them and loves them, he's an angel giving grace

Mother in a Tree

A woman had a baby in a tree
In the middle of a catastrophe
In the middle of the end of her world
A woman had a baby in a tree.

A woman became a mother in the motherland
Her present condition did not break her will
The elements did not deter her
Mother Nature could not stop Motherhood.
A woman became a mother in the motherland.

A strong woman refused to quit and refused to die
There was no I.V.
no fetal monitor
no epidural
There were no 10-year Doctors to assist with delivery
no mid-wives
no breast feeding nurses
There were no disposable diapers
And no incubators with heat lamps
There was only a strong woman who refused to quit and
    refused to die

A woman had a baby in a tree
A strong woman
Who refused to quit and refused to die had a baby in a tree
So a continent of Kings and Queens could be born

God Rest Her Soul

1 Cor 15: 55–57
55—O death, where is thy sting? O grave, where is thy victory?
56—The sting of death is sin; and the strength of sin is the law.
57—But thanks be to God, which giveth us the victory through
*   our Lord Jesus Christ.*
—KJV Bible

An angel said...

God has rescued her soul...
A life of earthly labor
finally taken its toll and
no man can provide relief

Shocked, none of this
seemed to register.
I fell to my knees in disbelief
when what was to come
came to be!

I raised my head and
struggled to rise
determined to face my fears
fists rubbing back tears
in finality, confronting...Death

Filled with anger and emotion
at this final blow
wiping tears from my eyes...
I cry!

Fighting Death,
I've been biting and cursing,
been yelling and screaming
my fists pounding and heart bleeding…

Oh, how it hurts
oh how I—have—cried…
my ribs cramping feeling empty inside
and I couldn't stop
no matter how I tried.
Feelings clouding my thoughts
as skies opened wide
storming questions down, why?
Why Death…why?

But by and by as I bided my time
it was faith realized
that calmed this dark storm
despite tearing up;
yet still the sun shone.

It revealed an answer
that was always inside
a revelation that Death
truly has no pride
and though he may try
there's no soul can he have…
'Cause God is our master
and now she's by his side.

An angel said…

God has rescued her soul
only HE can provide relief
from life's earthly form
no toil, no more labor
she's now peaceful and calm
At peace, I cast off my grief

A genesis of faith
in God to abide
and with that knowledge
I felt a warmth deep inside
a warmth from pure joy
that grew as I cried
joy growing from faith
that God will provide,
and eventually that joy
shows itself in hearts open wide

Tears of joy in reflecting the past
smiles for the memories
the good times that last
times with family, coworkers and friends
smiles for knowing her goodness.
Knowing that GRACE lives on within!

Love on North 33rd Street

Love is the old gas stove in the corner of the kitchen
The stove that needs to be lit by long box—stick matches
Something is always cooking from the moment you wake up
    till you go to bed
Snapped green beans, pan corn bread, peas, collards with ham
    hocks and yams...
Or a chicken, ham or a turkey glowing in the oven
Or a lemon cake; peach cobbler with dumplings; or rice
    pudding;
and the stove is always clean

Love is that black cast-iron skillet
The big one so heavy it takes two hands to hold steady
The one for frying fish, the wings and the pork chops,
especially the pork chops.
The one you care for by scrubbing it clean
Then oiling it back up with a dip of the grease from the cof-
    fee can on the stove

Love is hot rolls from scratch, without a recipe
Kneaded by hand, rolled with a wooden pin
Rolled on waxed paper, lightly sprinkled with flour
Rolls that wake you up with their aroma, aroma so strong you
    can taste them
Rolls that don't need butter, but you spread it heavy anyway
So the butter drips with each bite you take

Love is fresh tea made in a big glass pitcher
Lots of sugar, a couple wedges of lemon and a ton of ice
The sound the wooden spoon makes as it hits the side

is like a musical triangle screaming "come and get it."
Getting hypnotized by the view of the tea leaves and sugar
 spinning in a whirlpool
then floating and settling quietly back to the bottom like a
 shaken snow scene

Love is the talk you get before the walk to get your own
 switch
After you stepped on the flowers, left the porch, or pulled
 down the clothes line
For doing all those other things you knew you weren't sup-
 posed to do
You know better!
It's the sting of the switch on your legs or hands when you try
 to block
It's the hugs that make the hurt go away when it's all over…
Love is the walk back into the kitchen,
For a big glass of tea and that last piece of cake.

Only Love

Have you ever looked up
and counted each star
Or caught lightning bugs
in mayonnaise jars
Have you ever wanted to leave
but couldn't let go
Have you ever cared so much
you rarely said no

Have you ever been hungry
but shared your last bite
Have you ever been sleeping
and woke to calm someone's fright
Have you seen lots of sunsets
and still stare in awe
Or couldn't wait for that someone
to walk through the door

Have you ever been mad
but shut tight your lips
Or maybe…argued lightly
to give in a bit
'Cause you know in the end
making up's the best part
and no matter what happens
You're tied at the heart

Breath lost on contact
from the adrenaline push
Heart to head pounding
from the excitement and rush

Light-headed giggles and
smiles growing wide
and nothing else matters
but us side by side

Then yes…
There is only Love!

Never Cried

I have been going to funerals all my life. Death is a part of growing up. Friends, family, and associates; I've seen quite a few people buried, I know a lot who have died, and while I may have been misty eyed...I never cried.

Every Sunday at Sunday School we were reminded that Jesus died for us...to save our souls, and as painful as it looked in the books or in that stained glass mural behind the pulpit...We all learned to deal with it, Death!

Remember the day you sent your first goldfish down the bowl to his watery heaven or when your mom took Fluffy, Blackie, or Spot for that ride of no return. I never got to go but I was told they were going to a better place. Hell, even Bambi and Mufassa helped us realize that the good die too. We learned that Death was going to be walking side by side with happiness just waiting for us to get a bit too giddy.

I can remember watching my great grandma age practically before my eyes as my mother provided care for her. Walking throughout our house with her walker, watching her clothes seemingly grow on her, becoming too big. I saw an aunt go from a thriving energetic example of education and achievement to become bed-ridden and sullen. One day when she didn't open the door, I climbed up on the fire escape and looked into her window. I swear she looked at me with pleading eyes and outstretched arms. She had been there for me and there was nothing I could do.

I saw the EMS take another aunt from the house on a still and bitter winter night. The lights from the ambulance seemed to make noise as I watched them chase into and around the room through the window. I later saw my aunt in the hospital, shortly after her last breath. Her mouth was slightly open as if to tell me something quietly in my ear, as if she had more to say, as if she wanted to tell me one last thing! As if!

I witnessed those shells that were loving, energetic, and full of abundant life; emptied of their souls. And the minister said, "Death be not proud, they have gone to a better place." I was hurt, I felt tremendous loss and while I may have been misty eyed...I never cried.

My grandma made me get a switch from the switch bush in front of her house when I needed it. She scolded my nursery school teachers when they told me I couldn't sing with the class because I couldn't hold a tune. My grandma never let me leave her house without taking some of the rolls she made. My grandma held my children and bounced them on her knee. She gave them nicknames and sang to them, and when the world was wrong, my grandma made it right, she made things ok for them, just like she did for me. It was all ok till I got the call. The call that told me my grandma died.

I've been going to funerals all my life, but never cried...Death is a part of growing up. Friends, family, and associates; I've seen quite a few people buried, I know a lot who have died, and while I may have been misty eyed...I never cried.

I never cried till my grandma died.

About the Author

Photo by J. Motomal

Anthony P. Johnson is a Corporate Marketing Manager by day and a multiple personality poet and writer at night. He holds a degree in Speech and Theatre from North Carolina A&T State University and has worked in Sales and Public Relations. He has been featured at several spoken word venues in New Jersey.

"That's It!" is his first published collection.

He proudly calls New Jersey home.

For more information, please contact us at: iecomm@hotmail.com

Made in the USA
Lexington, KY
05 July 2014